Your Best Life

Creating Wealth with What You Have Today!

Tiffiny Traylor

All rights reserved. Without limiting the rights under copyright reserved above. No part of this book may be reproduced into retrieval system, or transmitted in any form, or by any means (electronic, mechanical, photocopying, recording, or otherwise) without the prior written consent from the author except brief quotes used in reviews, interviews, or magazines.

Your Best Life: Creating Wealth with what you have Today
Copyright © 2019 by Tiffiny Traylor
502030LifeStyle@gmail.com

About the Author

My name is Tiffiny Traylor, and I have 15+ years' experience in the Finance Industry. My passion is telling all who will listen about the importance of saving money for your current and future lifestyle options. Presently, I have obtained years of personal financial success in my life by trial and error. I would love to share with you the simple step-by-step money management strategies that I have implemented. Remember, when you have/save money, you also have options/freedom.

Let's take a look through my life, and the journey I traveled to get to my current financial state. In my youth, I spent money every weekend because I felt like I worked hard, therefore, I deserved to have fun! I only hurt myself because it put me in a cycle of spending money for my 'wants', and then borrowing money (payday loans) for my 'needs.' I began to feel continually stressed and changed my ways. I wouldn't let myself ask for anymore payday loans.

Shortly after, I made another wrong decision. I thought I deserved a new car. Consequently, I spent my disposable income on car payments, in lieu of putting it in savings. My huge mistake was not realizing, I was letting stuff (car payments, shopping, eating-out etc.) get in the way of saving for life's emergencies (family, medical, employment etc.) and retirement. Only until I desired a life of abundance, and the desire to have more in life, did I no longer live paycheck-to-paycheck. I realized that if I didn't make certain changes, I would always be a victim of debt. I made the decision to create a budget and stick to it. My next step was to clean up my credit. Thereafter, I began to save money for an emergency fund (8 months of expenses). Lastly, I started saving for retirement. By taking one step at a time and celebrating my accomplishments along the way, I achieved my financial goals – finally!

Please understand that it is not easy to get to this financial position. If it were easy, everyone would have money in the bank, a healthy retirement account, and live totally debt free. Unfortunately, that is not the situation for most people because delayed gratification is unpopular.

Just remember, the challenge is never greater than your will to take control of your life!

If you would like to contact me, I would love to hear from you.

502030LifeStyle@gmail.com

Dedication

This is dedicated to my mother, Ruthia Traylor. Thank you for your example and strength throughout the years. Today, I am the product of all the financial successes and failures that you have overcome. I celebrate you and thank God for you!

Introduction

The goal of this book is to help you live on less than what you make. It may sound simple, but many people do not see that as the avenue to obtaining wealth. If you make $20,000 a year, then you must live on less than that amount. If you make $50,000 a year, then you must live on less than that amount. No matter the amount of your paycheck, you will find yourself in debt if your outgo is more than your income. You may struggle with thoughts like, "I make only this much money, but I desire to buy this nice car." Many famous people have acquired tremendous wealth only to lose it all because they spent every dime of their earnings. One day, you will retire and be unable to maintain the particular revenue stream to which you grew accustomed. Therefore, having a healthy *Net Worth* is vital in order for you to maintain a comfortable lifestyle in your second chapter of life. Your assets (how much you own), minus your debt (what you owe), equals your *Net Worth*.

The first step you must take in order to have a healthy *Net Worth* is to create a *Budget* for yourself. The second step is to clear up your debt. Your goal is to be *Debt Free* and to stay that way. The third step is to save for an *Emergency Fund*, and your fourth step is to save for *Retirement*. At this point, you will be ready for additional *Investments* - cash only of course. You now know the steps to take, but the challenge can be in taking that first one. Don't worry; I will walk you through every step!

Table of Contents

Chapter 1 Budget Equals Wealth 1

Chapter 2 He Said, She Said 9

Chapter 3 You Can Be Debt Free 17

Chapter 4 Emergency Fund ASAP..21

Chapter 5 Investments Made Easy...27

Chapter 6 Time and Goal Management....................................31

Chapter 7 Takeaways...35

Chapter 8 25 Career Options 39

Appendix 47

Chapter 1
Budget Equals Wealth

They Say: "I don't make enough money to budget; I just pay bills."
Truth: Anyone who has an income should have a budget.

Creating a workable budget is the first and most important step in building your wealth. In order to budget, you must record the amount of money needed to pay for your expenses and subtract it from your monthly income. Every month you should know the total of all your bills and the entirety of your current income. If you have expenses that you cannot afford with your income, you now have the challenge to make smarter choices regarding your purchases. When you take into account the amount required for your housing, food, transportation, etc. - you control your expenses, rather than allowing them to control you.

Budget Monthly or by Pay Period
It is necessary to determine if your budget will be bi-weekly or monthly. When making a list of all your *Expenses*, you

must remember that your *Income* is your take-home pay minus the deduction of healthcare and retirement.

Begin your budget by dividing your income into these 3 categories, which are the Finance industry standards:

- 50% Expenses - Charity/tithing, housing, food, electric, water, transportation, insurance, etc.
- 20% Savings – Unless you need to pay off debt.
- 30% Lifestyle – Shopping, travel, entertainment, sports, etc. (unless you need to pay off debt first)

For Example: $2,000 Income
50% Expense = $1,000
20% Savings = $400
30% Lifestyle = $600
(Applies to income of 2,000 per month or 2,000 per week.)

Analyze your *Budget* to see if it lines up with the guidelines provided. If it doesn't, please adjust accordingly in order to maximize your *Wealth Goals*. It will take all of these aforementioned categories to build a life of financial success.

Expense Breakdown
On the following pages are two budgets that present examples of the *Wrong Budget* and the *Right Budget*. Take note that your goal is to have a "zero based budget" at the end of every month by applying every dollar to each line item. If your *Housing* is "over budget," you will be drowning in debt until you make changes to control the cost. If your *Expenses* are "over budget," that will keep you

in debt. If your *Lifestyle* is "over budget," you guessed it - that too will keep you in debt. Therefore, let's dive into this life-changing *BUDGET*, and get you pointed in the right direction.

Wrong Budget

Income $3,333	1st PayPeriod	2nd PayPeriod
Giving	166.5	166.5
Rent/ Mortgage	~~500~~	~~500~~
Food	200	200
Utilities	75	
Gas	75	75
Insurance		75
Car Payment	500	
Credit Cards		300
Loans	50	150
Expenses	1,566.50	1,466.50
Saving	*$0*	*$0*
Lifestyle	~~125.00~~	~~225.00~~
Total Expense	1,691.50	1,691.50
Income	1,666.50	1,666.50
Balance	(25.00)	(25.00)

Annual Saving $0

Need to decrease Rent/ Mortgage. Take lifestyle budget and add it to the regular car, credit cards and loans payments to pay-off Debts.

Right Budget

Income $3,333	1st PayPeriod	2nd PayPeriod
Giving	166.5	166.5
Rent/ Mortgage	300	300
Food	200	200
Utilities	75	
Gas	91.75	91.75
Insurance		75
Car Payment	$0	$0
Credit Cards	$0	$0
Loans	$0	$0
Expenses	833.25	833.25
Saving	*333.30*	*333.30*
Lifestyle	499.95	499.95
Total Expense	1,666.50	1,666.50
Income	1,666.50	1,666.50
Balance	0	0

Annual Saving $7,999.20

Because of No Debt, you have the ability to Build Wealth

Savings Breakdown

Ask yourself the following questions:

- What are my short-term *Saving Goals*? One of your short-term goals could be debt repayment. An average short-term goal is 6 to 18 months.
- What are my long-term *Financial Goals*? A common long-term goal is the purchase of a home. An average long-term goal takes from 2 to 6 years to achieve.
- What can I change in order to achieve my *Saving Goals*? When you have a clear view of your *Budget*, you have the ability to see the changes you can make in your spending habits. Saving for your future will finally be possible.

  For example, if your electric bill is less than expected, throw that into your *Savings*. If your grocery bill is less than expected, throw that into your *Savings* as well. Your *Budget* gives you the ability to know what money is available to contribute to your Savings in order to create "*Extra Savings*."

Track Expenses to Increase Savings

Maintaining a log of your *Expenses* each month will give you the ability to make cost-effective decisions. For instance, you should review your insurance premiums. If your insurance is increasing at the time of renewal, you should get quotes from other insurance companies. Many policyholders are unaware that they can change their policies at any time. If you find a more cost-effective policy, even after you renew, you are still able to cancel the original one and keep the new policy. However, please purchase the new policy *BEFORE* you cancel the original policy. It is the same with your Electric Company if you live in a state that allows you to choose your electric provider. There are always companies willing to have you as a customer. Look at your rates per usage and make a cost-effective choice. Lastly, it is wise to look for more affordable cell phone plans. There is always a cellular company that can provide a savings deal. Some people find a month-to-month cell phone plan is better than signing a contract.

When You've Got It

When you know exactly how much you have to spend, you won't always spend your entire amount. Whenever cash is leftover, move it to your *Savings*. You are now beginning to *Budget* - the fabulous tool that allows you to build up your *Savings*. Budgeting can be addictive. Once you see your money at work for you, you will want more. Budgeting is smart! By lowering your expenses, you will see your money grow which gives you the ability and the desire to save more. Therefore, work your *Budget*, and it will be your greatest tool in *Wealth Building*.

Ch. 1 - Financial Muscle Exercises

1. Do you currently use a budget?
2. Is your budget the "Right Budget" or the "Wrong Budget"?
3. What are your short-term goals? Your long-term goals?

Notes

Chapter 2
He Said, She Said

They Say: "We will never be able to agree on a budget."
Truth: If you don't agree on a budget, the relationship will suffer. *It Can Be Done!*

Let's talk about your "family" goals.
1. Do you want financial security for your loved ones?
2. Do you want to reduce money stress?
3. Are you able to temporarily sacrifice your wants and needs to attain this goal?
4. Will you both actively participate in your monthly budget process?
5. Are you serious about being dedicated to this process?

Hopefully all of your answers are "YES".

Having a willing partner to keep you accountable to this process is key. Having an unwilling partner will undermine it and make it difficult to accomplish your goals.

Budgeting on your own is a one person show, however, budgeting as a couple who combines their income can be twice as challenging. It is not easy to move from the mindset of providing for yourself and catering to your own wants and needs, to balancing that with the wants and needs of your spouse. Before planning out your 'shared budget', spend time together discussing the pros and cons of your spending. If your spouse rejects this idea or views it as unnecessary, you will need to discover any underlying problems that would prevent this important discussion.

Please don't think your lack of income today predicts your lack of income tomorrow. You must *Play the Game to Know the Game*. The income you have now will continually increase over time if you make wise decisions. It is necessary to learn how to make good use of what you have and to continue that behavior because it will greatly benefit you later. The only way to understand your *Savings Options* is to use … a *Budget*! No matter your income level, I hope now you understand and take a special interest in creating a workable *Budget* for yourself.

Modify Your Expectations

If you and your partner are married, you may need to change your financial expectations in order for both of you to be on the same page. One of you may be used to living lighter and saving most of what he or she earns, while the other may desire a better living space which would require use of some of your savings. The most important part of budgeting, whether single or married, is prioritizing your needs over your wants. Also, if one of you is burdened with a considerable amount of debt, devise a plan together that will pay it off without causing a lot of financial strain. Being forced to sit down and talk about each other's financial situations helps both of you to see the bigger picture. More often than not, the conversation will change from strictly 'money talk' to how to accomplish your dreams, how to contribute any extra money to savings, and how to generate extra income. Being able to discuss your budget is both financially and emotionally beneficial.

It has been reported that approximately 70% of couples have arguments about their finances - a subject that tops all other common relationship problems. Not surprisingly, the number one leading cause of divorce is over *Finances*. Most financial disagreements occur because the two in the relationship are not working together toward a common goal.

An example could be that one of you may be inclined to resent your spouse for spending too much money on video games, while the other spends what they believe is an exorbitant amount on beauty products and vice versa. It is important to recognize that you both have different interests that may cost more or less than the other.

Discussing money issues early and often in a relationship is helpful to ensure that you both are working together to accomplish your goals. Creating a budget is the best way to prevent tension caused by finances between the two of you, and to ultimately bring you closer as a couple.

It is also very important to learn how to compromise. Listen to your partner to understand what is important to them. Be sure that you both have a certain amount of money set aside to spend on the things that are most important to each of you. As long as each partner uses their given amount wisely, there will be no reason to fight about how the money is spent.

Track Your Spending Together

You both need to put an effort into tracking your spending. The most effective tracking method is a *Weekly Budget*. In the process of creating your budget, you can discuss your current financial situation versus the changes you want to make for the future. Further, you can discuss how much you have left in each spending area and expenses that may occur in the future. By budgeting together, you can change your spending categories as needed.

When you begin to track your spending, it is a good idea to use cash in order to limit cost. On the first day of the week, withdraw the amount of cash you will need for that week's expenses. When the money is gone – it's gone. Surprisingly, making the conscious decision to limit your costs somehow shows you that you didn't need as much as you originally thought. As you get used to basing your spending habits on your budget, you can change your meeting time to bi-weekly or monthly. One way to keep track of your spending habits is by using a spreadsheet program or a low-cost (possibly free) budgeting app for your phone.

Your meetings will get shorter and will be just as effective as you both become more comfortable with following your budget. Additionally, when you are in a meeting together, it is important to remain calm. If one spouse makes a mistake, you gently find a solution and move forward. It does not help to dwell on mistakes or to continually bring them up.

The weekly budget meeting is a major component in getting your budget to work. There are apps designed specifically to help you budget like one that can give you an update on how much is being spent if you are shopping in two different places.

Tips:

1. If you or your spouse do not want to combine finances, then it is imperative that you set up a budget for all of the household expenses. A financial counselor can provide a calm environment and sound advice to assist both of you.
2. If you are eventually going to get married, set up an individual household budget until the two of you are ready to combine your finances.
3. The budget that you create should have your financial goals outlined as you continually add to your savings. (cash for car, home, investment, etc.)
4. Go on dates even if they are 'cheap' dates. Bonding is an area of your relationship that must not suffer while you are saving for your future.

Beware of Being Tired, 'Hangry', or in a Hurry

Have you ever tried to have a serious conversation when you were tired, 'hangry' (hungry + angry) or in a hurry for an appointment? If you have, then you know those talks never turn out well. Therefore, plan a time when both of you are rested, full, and relaxed. One of the best times to discuss important topics is after a meal. Make sure to plan a time to talk when no one has to get to an appointment or right before bedtime. Also, turn off your cell phones. This conversation does not need any distractions.

Honesty Is the Best Policy

Everyone has a certain idea of how money should be saved or spent. Mostly, our parents shaped us when we were very young. We watched how they handled their money. We observed how they either made us wait for the things we wanted until we could afford them, or how they gave us whatever we wanted. Because of your family history, one of you may be more of a saver than a spender. As in most relationships, no one always agrees on everything, but taking the time to discuss your finances creates trust with one another which is the best foundation for a relationship! Being honest with one another about your spending habits prevents you from hurting each other's feelings now and in the future.

Define Your Goals

What is most important to both of you in life - not just financially? What are your *Dreams*? During these discussions you may realize that you want to make a career change. You also may discover that you want to relocate to a different climate, take a dream vacation, or join a recreational club. Together, you are deciding on *Spending* your money on an idea that makes you both excited. Communication is a key factor in having a fulfilling relationship and in successfully managing your finances, paying off a debt, taking that vacation or going to every concert within driving distance. Those goals will drive your decisions of how to spend your money.

Differences in Incomes

A popular insecurity and point of contention for many couples is when one has a larger income than the other. This can be remedied by a lesson in sharing. If you are in debt, it will take both incomes to resolve the debt. When debit is out of the picture, you both will share the available savings. Paying off your debt allows you to make major life decisions that benefit each of you. The goal is to create a budget, pay off debt, save for emergencies, and invest for the future TOGETHER.

Ch. 2 – Financial Muscle Exercises

1. Does your budget satisfy the both of you?
2. Do you have weekly/bi-weekly/monthly budget meetings?
3. Have you made a specific, detailed list of goals?
4. Are you ready to make YOUR dreams a reality?

Chapter 3
You Can Be Debt Free

They say: "I have way too many debts on my credit report, so it will be there forever."
Truth: Anyone who has an income and time, has the ability to be free of debt.

Make Your List and Check It Twice
Being *Debt Free* is a major step to *Wealth Building*. Make a list of *ALL* of your debts ranging from the smallest to the greatest. Take the *Surplus* from your monthly *Budget* to pay down the smallest debt. Next, pay the second one off. Continue this trend and your debt will eventually be gone. Commonly, one of people's largest debts, other than buying a home, is a car loan. We spend a considerable sum of our income on car payments. It seems that as soon as we pay off one loan, we celebrate by buying a new car. Continuing to purchase expensive items while paying off debt is counterproductive. Furthermore, many of us also have student loans to repay. Student loans can be overwhelming, but if you just stay the course you will

eventually pay them off. Try to remember my catchphrase: *One by one and it will be done.* The *Goal* is not to have a debt line item on your *Budget*, but to become *DEBT FREE* and to stay debt free.

Non-negotiables

When looking at your spending, there are two areas that are non-negotiables: *Credit cards* and *Car payments*. You cannot build wealth if you are chained with these payments every month. These are not an option for you. Are you aware that the average credit card payment is $300 a month, and the average new car payment is $515 a month? When you add those together you could be saving $815 a month and $9780 annually. At this point, your Savings in 3 years will be $29,340. In 6 years, it will be $58,680! *YOU CAN CHANGE YOUR LIFE*! So, get moving and pay off your credit cards and close those accounts. Keeping them open will tempt you to use them again. Also, after paying off your car, do not get another car payment. Instead, drive your current car and make repairs as needed. Take the time to save for another previously owned 'new to you' car and pay with cash. If you can't pay with cash, it is not worth *IT*.

Should Have, Would Have, Could Have

I wish I had known in my 20's what I know now about personal finance. In our youth, we are given student debt, credit cards, and car notes as a normal order of life. What if you were given the *Wealth Building Tools* that could give you financial security? No matter your age, it is never too late to build wealth with the money you are currently earning. However, do not wait to take action. *Do It NOW!* It takes *Dedication* and *Self-Control* to tell your friends and family that you can't go out shopping or take trips with them. You can always do that when you have cash to spend after paying off your debt. It will take *Commitment* to make a plan, to see it through, and *Time* to get out of the debt that you accumulated over months or years. Just understand that your future could be *Full* of possibilities. It's true! Whatever you want, you can have - *IF You Work Your Plan*.

Be a Giver

Most people have heard the saying, *Give and it shall be given to you*. When you give of your resources and time, a more fulfilled and abundant life will be opened up to you. If you are a church member - *give and it shall be given to you*. If you are interested in a non-profit business - *give and it shall still be given*. If there are local volunteer opportunities - *give and it shall be given*. Lending a helping hand to those in need will allow us to take time to reflect on our own lives. Whatever life has dealt you, there is someone worse off than you. Therefore, be an extension of love and charity. You will receive more than you could ever *GIVE*.

Ch. 3 – Financial Muscle Exercises

1. Have you made a list of your debts ranging from the smallest to the greatest?
2. What is your smallest debt? What is your greatest debt?
3. Are you excited about the estimated savings of $58,680 on cars and credit cards?

4. Are you giving back to a charity?

Chapter 4
Emergency Fund ASAP

They say: "I don't see a way that I can save 8 months of Expenses!"
Truth: *You Can Do It* - one step at a time!

How to Create an Emergency Fund

Try to envision the stress that will melt away from you when you're able to look at your growing *Savings Account*. 20% seems like such a small number, but it is enormous when it comes to *Building Wealth*. In order to create an *Emergency Fund*, take your monthly *Budget* and multiply it by 8 months. This is a limited budget because the expenses that you have while gainfully employed will be less than if you were unemployed. For example, you may be able to save on transportation and food because you aren't traveling back and forth to a job. If you are unable to save 20% of your *Income*, you will need to adjust your *Expenses*. You may need to make some sacrifices to adjust your *Lifestyle Budget* in order to achieve this *Goal*. Understand that it will take approximately 1 to 1 ½ years to complete your *Emergency Fund*, however, it is necessary. When life happens to you, an *Emergency Fund* gives you time to adjust.

Special note: Save your EF in a Money Market Savings account for safe keeping. Don't mix funds with your checking account. Your local banker can assist you in setting up this account.

15 Reasons Why You NEED an Emergency Fund

1. **Loss of Employment** - An Emergency Fund allows you to seek the employment that you desire - not feeling the pressure to take the first job offer that you receive.

2. **Start a New Business** – Use your Emergency Fund to pay expenses from leaving a job to owning a business. In business, you will always have unexpected expenses – plan for it.

3. **Pregnancy** - How exciting, however, it wasn't expected. With an Emergency Fund, you will feel better about the expenses that come along with a pregnancy and you will be prepared in case your employer doesn't offer parental leave pay.

4. **A Medical Emergency** - Having money for a medical emergency feels much better than watching those enormous bills stack up on your desk.

5. **Transportation Problems -** You're ready for work, but your car is not. That's okay because you have the money for repairs and a car rental.

6. **Your Hours Were Cut at Work -** Working fewer hours equals less pay, but now you have funds to fall back while you seek a better job.

7. **A Friend Needs Help and a Place to Stay -** You are able to care for yourself and others when you have an Emergency Fund in place.

8. **Your Identity is Stolen -** This can wreak havoc on your ability to pay your bills, access your accounts, etc. While all of this is getting sorted out, you have cash on hand to help you get through all of this mess.

9. **Unexpectedly, You Need to Relocate because of unsafe weather conditions -** Because you thought ahead, you have the ability to quickly find a new place to live and pay for any moving expenses you may incur.

10. **Your Partner has been Unfaithful or (you are fearful and you want to stay somewhere other than your home) -**.You are able to leave when you choose with no questions asked.

11. **You Have the Job Offer you Always Wanted, but the Pay Isn't There Yet -** You have the ability to take that job, and wait for the salary increase.

12. **Treatment Centers -** Addictions are a part of life for some people, and if you have the funds you are able to head this disaster off before it destroys you or those you love.

13. **Attending a Funeral in Another Country -** This can be costly, but with your fund you are able to grieve the loss of your friend or family member with others who loved them as well.

14. **A Major Household Expense (AC/HVAC, plumbing, electrical, etc.) –** These are very costly items that you will pay without missing a beat.

15. **Accepting a New Job in Another State -** You are able to take this job, because you have the funds to relocate, whereas many in this situation would lose the opportunity.

Emergency Funds Change Your Life

All of these events, and many more, can cause an otherwise stable financial situation to quickly collapse into chaos, forcing you to tap your credit (hard). If you're lucky, your emergency doesn't also coincide with a moment where you have employment issues and household expenses that require this kind of resource.

However, after your *Emergency Fund* is in place, guess what? Your conversations will change. If you find that your job is unfulfilling, you have 8 months to find another *Income Path*. In the unfortunate event that you or a loved one has a serious illness, an *Emergency Fund* will afford you the medical care that you need and deserve. Lastly, if a romantic relationship doesn't work out it's not the end of *YOUR LIFE*. When you have options - you got *Options*!

Ch. 4 – Financial Muscle Exercises

1. Do you have an Emergency Fund?
2. Use your budget to calculate your Emergency Fund.
3. How long will it take you to acquire a Fund?
4. What spending habits can you change in order to save a few extra dollars to put into an Emergency Fund?
5. How important is it to have an Emergency Fund in your life?

Chapter 5
Investments Made Easy

They say: "I don't want to save for retirement. I may die tomorrow."
Truth: What if you don't die? Do you want to work until you die? Surely not! Retire and live a life of leisure.

In order to make sound investments, the following steps are necessary to achieve this goal.

Step 1: FREE Money
If your employer has a 401K retirement plan match - take it. Usually, when you contribute 1% to 5% of your income, an employer will also contribute up to 5%. The total investment into your retirement fund, which you can use for more investments, goes up to 10%. Whatever match your employer gives you - use that free money. The taxes will be deducted from your fund when you retire.

Step 2: BIG Money

After you acquire all of your 401K matching contributions from your employer, it is wise to invest in a Roth IRA. A Roth IRA (Roth Individual Retirement Account) is available through all financial services companies. The money you contribute to this fund will grow tax-free. Also, there is a wide variety of investment fund options. At retirement, 100% of the fund is yours.

The aforementioned investments will allow your money to multiply over time because of a wonderful concept called *Compound Interest*. With the power of Compound Interest, your money is reinvested. You purchase investments (stocks), and your investments make money (X 1); then you reinvest the money you make into additional investments (X 2). This process will continually happen with *Compound Interest*. In time, this concept enables you to attain *Wealth*.

Step 3: CA$H Investments

After retirement savings are set into place, you can move forward with additional investing. You are able to use the savings from your *Budget* to pay cash for investments. There could be a company that you would like to create/explore. Maybe you would like to add real estate to your investment portfolio or join a partnership where you would enjoy being a contributor. Life is exciting again because now you have a multitude of options to consider

Basically, you want to save and invest in order to reach your *Wealth Goals*. The rewards can be tremendous and you will have more money for family, leisure, retirement, or to pass on to the next generation. Maybe you don't have thousands just sitting there in your bank account, however, most of us have lunch money. Instead of eating out, take your lunch from home and start saving just $4/day for 300 days out of the year. Now you can save $1,200 and if invested you can earn at least 10% annually. *Compound Interest* will allow you to retire early if you continue to invest the same amount each year. If you are older and you don't have as much time to wait, double it to $8/day or more and watch it grow even faster!

Special Note: Research Investment/Retirement accounts with companies like Fidelity, Charles Schwab and Mutual of America for an account that fits you.

Ch. 5 – Financial Muscle Exercises

1. Have you started saving for Retirement? If not, which options are you considering?
2. Does your employer offer a 401k?
3. How important is retirement for you and your family?
4. After a retirement, account, what additional investments are you considering?

Chapter 6
Time and Goal Management

They say: "When I get off work, I'm too tired to research and start a business."
Truth: If it were easy, *EVERYBODY* would do it, build it, *AND* own it. Time, determination and passion are the key elements that will propel you toward success.

Opportunity
If you don't do anything else, please be ready to meet with me (opportunity) and consider these scenarios: If only I had been saving money; If only I had the money to fund career training; If only I had the money to open a business; If only I had the money for a down payment on a house. I promise, you can do it. I promise it will not be easy. I promise it will take time. I promise you will get stronger as you flex your financial muscle. I promise you will get there if you don't give up. Your mind will reach the goal before

you can touch IT.

What is the alternative?
None! There is no alternative. 7 out of 10 people are living paycheck to paycheck. Even if it takes you 3 years, 6 years or 9 years, *DO It*. Life is going to go on; why not make it the foremost vision for your *LIFE?* If you were guaranteed *SUCCESS* in 36 months, could you stay focused and on task long enough to see it materialize? Be honest. If success were easy… it wouldn't be called *Success*. I confidently proclaim that there is almost nothing I would not sacrifice to live a financially self-assured life.

Direct your Energy
What is it that you want to accomplish? Direct your time and energy toward it! Have a plan… work the plan! We all are on our way somewhere. What are you doing about your future? Have you mapped out the year with scheduled targets to meet? Calendar yourself confidently. Daily document your personal homework assignment. Then, set a reminder to review open tasks on the weekend.

A day becomes a week, a week becomes a month, and then you're on your way.

Make Something Out of Nothing
When your creative juices aren't flowing, just start doing something - anything! When ideas come to mind, take the time to write them down. Just the pure act of creating something is *Powerful*. We have the power to *Think, Process and Create*. So, go ahead and do it. Be your authentic self. You are so special and unique. Don't disappoint by not

showing the world your talents.

Opportunity
- **Option #1**: When you need $500 to start an online business – Getting on a budget and managing your money allows you to start. *Income, time and opportunity.*
- **Option #2**: When you need $1000 to buy into a partnership venture, you have the money saved to invest. *Income, time and opportunity.*
- **Option #3**: When you need $2000 to invest in education, which will increase your Net Worth, you have savings to fund it. *Income, time, and opportunity.*

Ch. 6 – Financial Muscle Exercises

1. Have you ever missed an opportunity because you didn't have the funds?
2. Do you have Short-Term Goals and detailed steps to accomplish them?
3. Do you have Long-Term Goals and detailed steps to accomplish them?

Chapter 7
Takeaways

Let Me Ask You a Question
What if you met two people, **Person A** and **Person B**, with whom you were interested in developing a relationship? Let's review your options.

1. **Person A** had an income of $50,000 and spent $50,000 a year in Expenses. $0 Net Worth.

2. **Person B** had an income of $30,000, and Saved $10,000 (33%) per year, for 5 years creating $50,000 in Savings. $50,000 Net Worth.

Based on the above facts, which one would be your best choice for a relationship? Choose wisely. Person B had the time and patience to direct his/her money and see it through to a successful end. After 5 years, Person B had amassed a nice Net Worth while Person A had $0 in his/her savings. Take note that Person A made $20,000 more than Person B. As you learn new concepts in this book, understanding the difference between your *Net Worth* and your *Income* is vital for you to have financial security and the lifestyle of your choosing. Your *Net Worth* is not the value of the items you purchase (i.e. $1,000,000 house). It is not your credit limit (i.e. unlimited credit cards). Your *Net Worth* is the amount of money you currently have (i.e. cash, savings & retirement) minus the amount you owe (i.e. mortgage, car, student loans, credit cards). If you have $100,000 and a total debt of $20,000, your *Net Worth* is $80,000.

The Twenties

In your 20's, you need to hit the ground running. As soon as you're employed, start a retirement account. You have the ability to save a small amount in your account and *Compound* it over time (45 years). Funding as little as $2,000 ($83 biweekly) a year for 8 years will accomplish a lot. At age 28, you have the option to stop investing. And at retirement, you will have $1,000,000+. How could this be? *Compound Interest*!

The Thirties

In your 30's, you will have the ability to focus on your *Passion*. Don't get distracted by spending traps that will keep you in debt. Pay cash for your purchases (i.e. cars, travel, shopping). If what you desire is more than your income, it's not worth the debt to get it now. So, *Save* and take the time to explore your *Passion*. What is it that makes you happy? Find out what you're designed to do. Success will follow after you discover your *Purpose*.

The Forties

In your 40's, you have *Options* as to a career or a different life direction. Do you want to continue with your career, or do you want to change fields? Is life what you have always wanted and needed? Do you want to live in another country? Take time to explore your income goals. Spend time to look at your retirement goals. Make sure you take advantage of all opportunities that are suitable for your life goals.

The Fifties

In your 50's, life's a dream! Your retirement should be tracking real-time, with 15 years to go. At this point, your mortgage payments should have ended. Now is the time to begin to look for alternative income options - whether in real estate or in hobbies that have become businesses. Maybe there is a charity or a non-profit organization that you want to support. Now is the time to plan and fund all of your ventures! Just picture yourself with a carefree life because you have no debts hanging over your head.

Today is the first day of the rest of your life. Make plans. *Budget* your income and *Seize Opportunities* to *Invest* your savings. *Spend* your *Time* achieving your *Goals*, and you can be *Debt-Free* while you are still young enough to enjoy the *Best Things in Life*!

Ch. 7 – Financial Muscle Exercises

1. Do you know your Net Worth? If not, calculate what you *Own* minus what you *Owe*.
2. According to your age group, do you feel that you are where you need to be financially?
3. Do you have the desire to start where you are now to build wealth?
4. Do you think that creating a *Budget* is the key to *Building Wealth*?

Chapter 8
25 Career Options No Degree Required

The following is a partial list of career paths that only require passion and desire to become successful. Many people have no idea of the number of jobs available to them in the marketplace.

1. **Armed Services**
   Navy, Airforce, Army, or Marines. The Only requirement - a HEART to serve. Lieutenant Junior Grade Median Pay - $42,000/yr., 2 yr. in the Navy - $49,000/yr., 3 yr. in the Navy - $56,000/yr., 4 years in the Navy - $58,000/yr.

2. **Firefighter**
   Veterans have the ability to enter into this career path, without a college degree. Median Salary for a Firefighter $49, 5000/yr.

3. **Emergency Medical Technician**
   EMT requires certification only. Salary for an EMT on average is $45,000/yr.

4. **Police Officer**
   Veterans have the ability to enter into this career path, without a college degree. Median Salary - $61,100/yr.

5. **Insurance Broker**
   For commercial/ business insurance. State license required only. It is suggested that independent insurance brokers – distinct from sales agents who are salaried to a single insurance company – earn considerably more. To apply for an Agent License, you need to be sponsored by an Agent or Broker, then complete a state required exam. Look up your states Department of Insurance for detailed information. Median Salary - $59,600/yr.

6. **Insurance Agent**
   Focusing on personal (auto/ home) and life & health insurance. State license required only. Salary ranges can vary widely depending on many important factors which include education, certifications, additional skills, and the number of years spent in your profession. To apply for an Agent License, you need to be sponsored by an Agent or Broker, then complete a state required exam. Look up your state's Department of

Insurance for detailed information. Median Salary - $50,500/yr.

7. **Claims Adjusters and Examiners**

   Claims adjusters, appraisers, examiners, and investigators evaluate insurance claims. To apply for an Adjuster's License, you need to be sponsored by an Agent or Broker, then complete a state required exam. Look up your state's Department of Insurance for detailed information. – Median Salary - $59,900/yr.

8. **IT Support Tech**

   Only requires a certificate (e.g. Microsoft) Median Salary - $47,000/yr.

9. **Chef**

   Self-taught or with a certificate. Common salaries for head chefs are between $50,000 and $100,000/yr., with the highest salaries awarded by the largest and most reputable properties.

10. **Interior Design**

    Self-taught or with a certificate the average interior designer can expect to make a base salary of around $50,000, but it may be closer to $65,000-$70,000 after all the additional perks and kickbacks are factored into it. And if you're a seasoned, self-employed designer with an impeccable reputation and a vast portfolio of amazing projects, you can easily flirt with the $100,000 mark.

11. **Visual Artist**
    Visual artist are self-taught or trained. A Fine Artist, including a Painter, Sculptor, or Illustrator usually gets an average pay level between $40,000 – $60,000, based on experience. Fine Artists, Including Painters, Sculptors, and Illustrators will usually earn - Median Salary - $53,000/yr.

12. **Singer**
    Music Artist – Self-taught or trained. In terms of payments to music creators per 1,000 streams, Apple comes out well ahead of Spotify and YouTube. Apple pays between $12 and $15 per 1,000 streams, whereas Spotify pays around $7 per 1,000 streams, and YouTube pays around $1.

13. **Music Producer**
    Self-taught or with a certificate. Beat Maker, or a Music Producer writes, arranges, produces and records songs for other artists or for their own projects. This Salary can be all over the map. Median Salary - $49,000/yr. to Salary Range: $25,000 to $1,000,000.

14. **Music (writer)**
    Self-taught or trained. Writers, Lyricists, and songwriters craft songs for another artist or their own projects in hopes of creating a hit. This career

salary is varied as well. Median Salary - $0 - $1,000,000.

15. Photographer

Self-taught or trained. **Average annual pay** for a Wedding Photographer in the United States is $107,875/yr. While annual salaries as high as $133,000 and as low as $78,000, the majority of Wedding Photographer's salaries currently range between $104,000 (25th percentile) to $125,000 (75th percentile) across the United States.

16. Professional Driver

The average salary for a Truck Driver is $73,833/yr. in the United States. Salary estimates are based on 1,393,290 salaries submitted anonymously to Indeed by Truck Driver employees, users, and collected from past and present job advertisements on Indeed in the past 36 months.

17. Author

Be it nonfiction or fiction - this is a great career if you're passionate about it and have something to _GIVE_ to the world. Salary range is unlimited, depending on the individual author and their popularity and sales only. I don't know about you, but Unlimited sounds like heaven to me!

18. Blogger

Use what you're passionate about to make a great living. One of the most common ways bloggers make money is through placing ads on their site. CPC/PPC Ads: Cost per click (also called pay per click) ads are usually banners that you place in your content or sidebar. Each time a reader clicks on the ad, you are paid for that click.

19. **Publicist**

    People with great people skills will excel in this career. Depending on the city or region, prices can vary, of course. What is typically universal, though, is that you'll get what you pay for–especially with an agency. Publicists range from $2,000 to $10,000 per month, $120,000 per year (and beyond), with the average in New York City hovering around $7,000 per month/$84,000 per year.

20. **Entrepreneur**

    Create the career you want. Make sure to include Love/ Passion/ Determination. If you love what you do for a living, that also gives life to others, MONEY will come! Try it and see. Median Salary - Unlimited $$$

21. **Purchasing agents, except wholesale, retail, and farm products**

    Purchase machinery, equipment, tools, parts, supplies, or services necessary for the operation of an establishment. Median Salary - $60,000/yr.

22. **First Line Supervisors of Construction Trades**

Directly supervise and coordinate activities of construction or extraction workers. Median Salary - $59,700/yr.

23. **Gas Plant Operators** - Control systems and do round checks to make sure everything is working properly. Median Salary - $61,000/yr.

24. **Aerospace Engineering Technician** Aerospace engineering and operations technicians operate and maintain equipment used in developing, testing, and producing new aircraft and spacecraft. Median Salary - $61,500

25. **Web Developer**
Design, Create, and Modify Websites. Median Salary - $62,500/yr.

Ch. 8 – Financial Muscle Exercises

1. From the list of careers, are there any employment requirements that surprised you?
2. Out of the 25 careers listed in this chapter, are there any that interest you? Which ones?
3. If you are currently in a fulfilling career, will you pass along these career titles to someone you know who is looking for employment?
4. Will you suggest this book to a friend, so they can be Debt Free and achieve their Financial Goals?

Appendix

Definitions

<u>Asset</u> - Something of value that you own.

<u>Appreciating assets</u> – Items such as real estate, stocks that have the potential of increasing in value and/or producing income.

<u>Depreciating assets</u> – Items such as cars, electronics that depreciates in value over time.

<u>Finance Portfolio</u> - The value of a grouping of financial assets such as real estate, stocks, bonds, commodities, currencies and cash equivalents, as well as their funds (401K, IRA, Roth IRA etc.)

<u>Net Worth</u> – Your financial value number. Assets minus liabilities (what you owe) equals net worth.

<u>Compound Interest</u> - is the addition of interest to the principal sum of deposit, or in other words, interest on interest. It is the result of reinvesting interest, rather than paying it out, so that interest in the next period is then earned on the principal sum plus previously accumulated interest.

<u>401(k) Plan</u> - This plan is a defined contribution plan where an employee can make contributions from his or her paycheck either <u>before or after-tax</u>, depending on the options offered in the plan. The contributions go into a 401(k) account, with the employee often choosing the investments based on options provided under the plan.

<u>IRA</u> - An Individual Retirement Account (IRA) is a government sponsored tax deferred personal retirement plan. Taxes on Traditional IRA contributions and earnings are deferred until the account owner takes a distribution from the IRA. When money is withdrawn from a Traditional IRA it is **taxed** as regular income.

<u>Roth IRA</u> - A retirement savings account that allows your money to grow tax-free. You fund a Roth with after-tax dollars, meaning you've already paid taxes on the money you put into it. In return for no up-front tax break, your money grows and grows tax free, and when you withdraw at retirement, you pay **no taxes**.

<u>Mutual Fund</u> - A company that pools money from many investors and invests the money in securities such as stocks, bonds, and short-term debt. The combined holdings of the mutual fund are known as its portfolio. Investors (you) buy shares in mutual funds (via 401k, IRA, Roth IRA).

NOTES

www.ingramcontent.com/pod-product-compliance
Lightning Source LLC
LaVergne TN
LVHW051512070426
835507LV00022B/3070